Togo Colouring Book

I0462674

It is well documented that, for many people (adults and children alike), colouring is a therapeutic, stress-relieving pastime.

What could be better, then, than colouring in images of the beautiful country of Togo in West Africa? Despite being one of the smallest countries in Africa, Togo has a vibrant culture, stunning countryside and interesting towns and villages, making it a great subject for a colouring book.

Unlike most other colouring books which are usually filled with whimsical and cartoon images, mine are full of real pictures.

In this case, the colouring pages were created from photographs I took during a Dragoman tour of West Africa. We spent several days in Togo, getting to know the people and learning about their way of life. Within this book, you will find images of Togolese village life including mosques, churches and schools. There are pictures of Lake Togo and rural Mount Klouto, as well as the busier towns of Togoville and Lomé. There is also an image of stunning bright batik scarves for sale by the road.

Grab your favourite pens or pencils and let your imagination and creativity run riot. I use high quality fine-tip felt pens for the details, and coloured pencils for the larger areas, but the choice is yours. Some people like to put a water colour wash across the whole picture before they begin. It's your creation. It's up to you!

Cut out your finished work and display it somewhere as in inspiration to travel further for longer, or as a reminder of places you've already been to.

Keep in touch with me at Happy Days Travel Blog or on social media:

@happydaystravelblog   @happydayswriter

Show me your creations, follow my travels and tell me about yours!

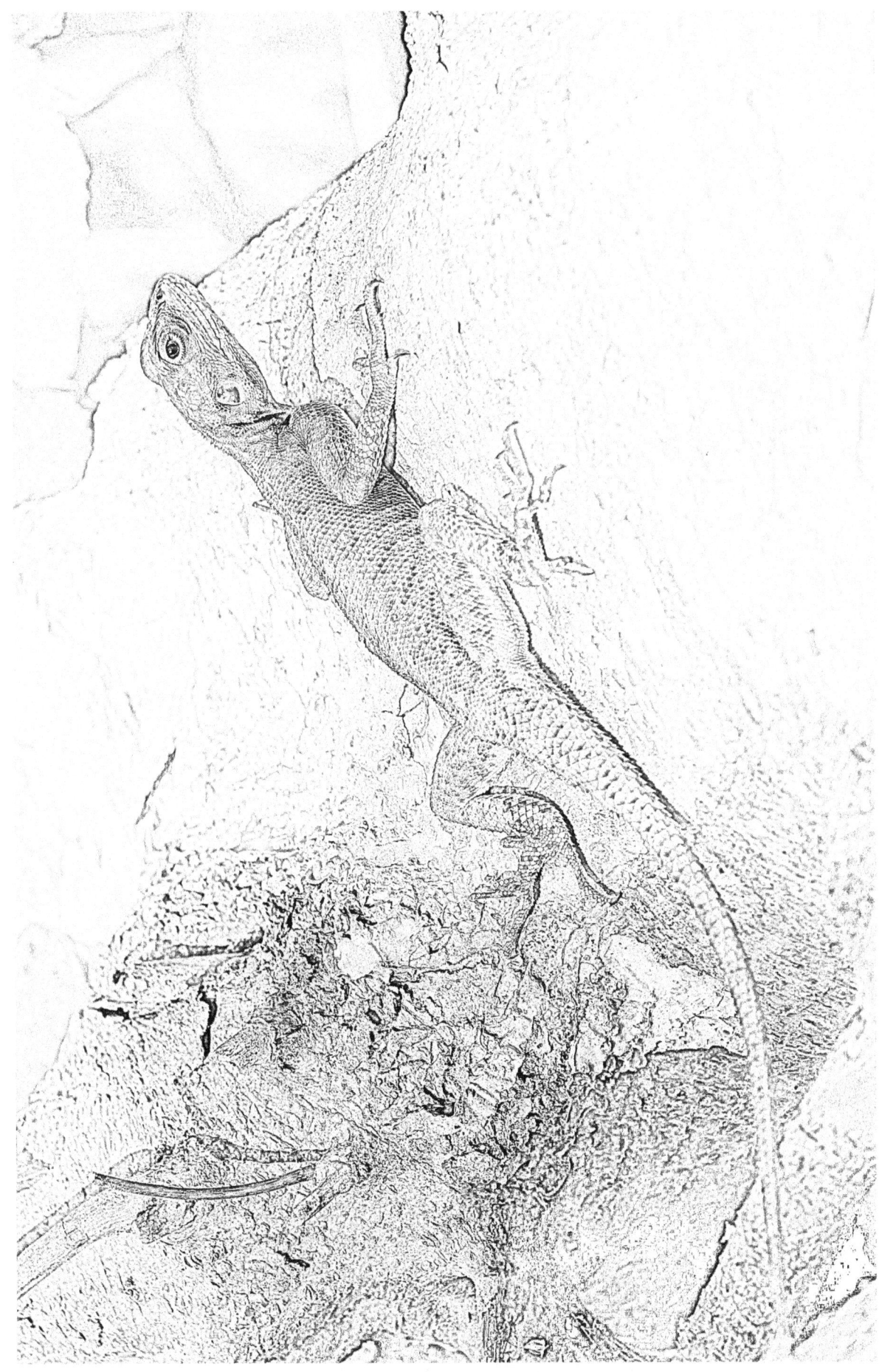

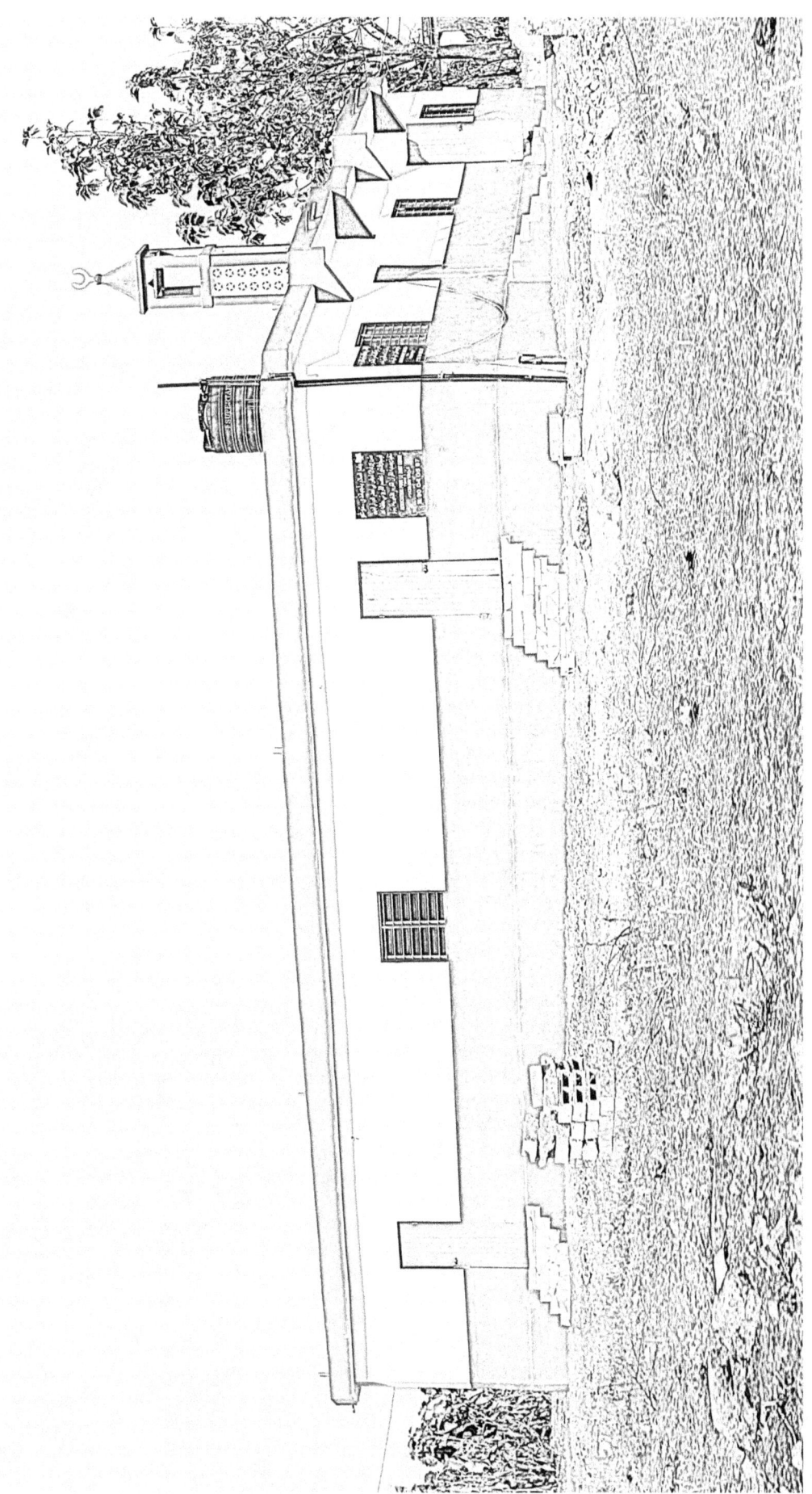

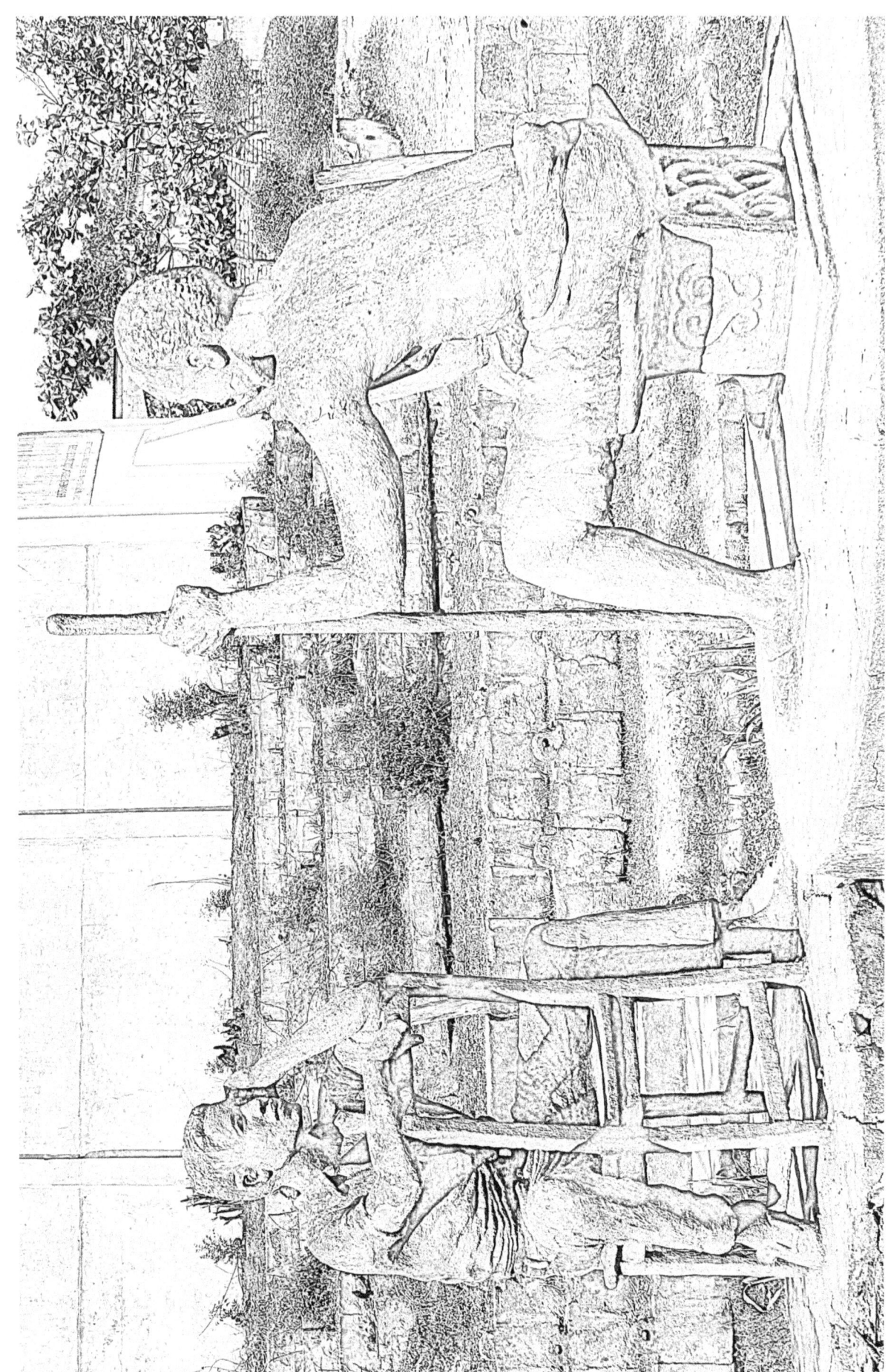

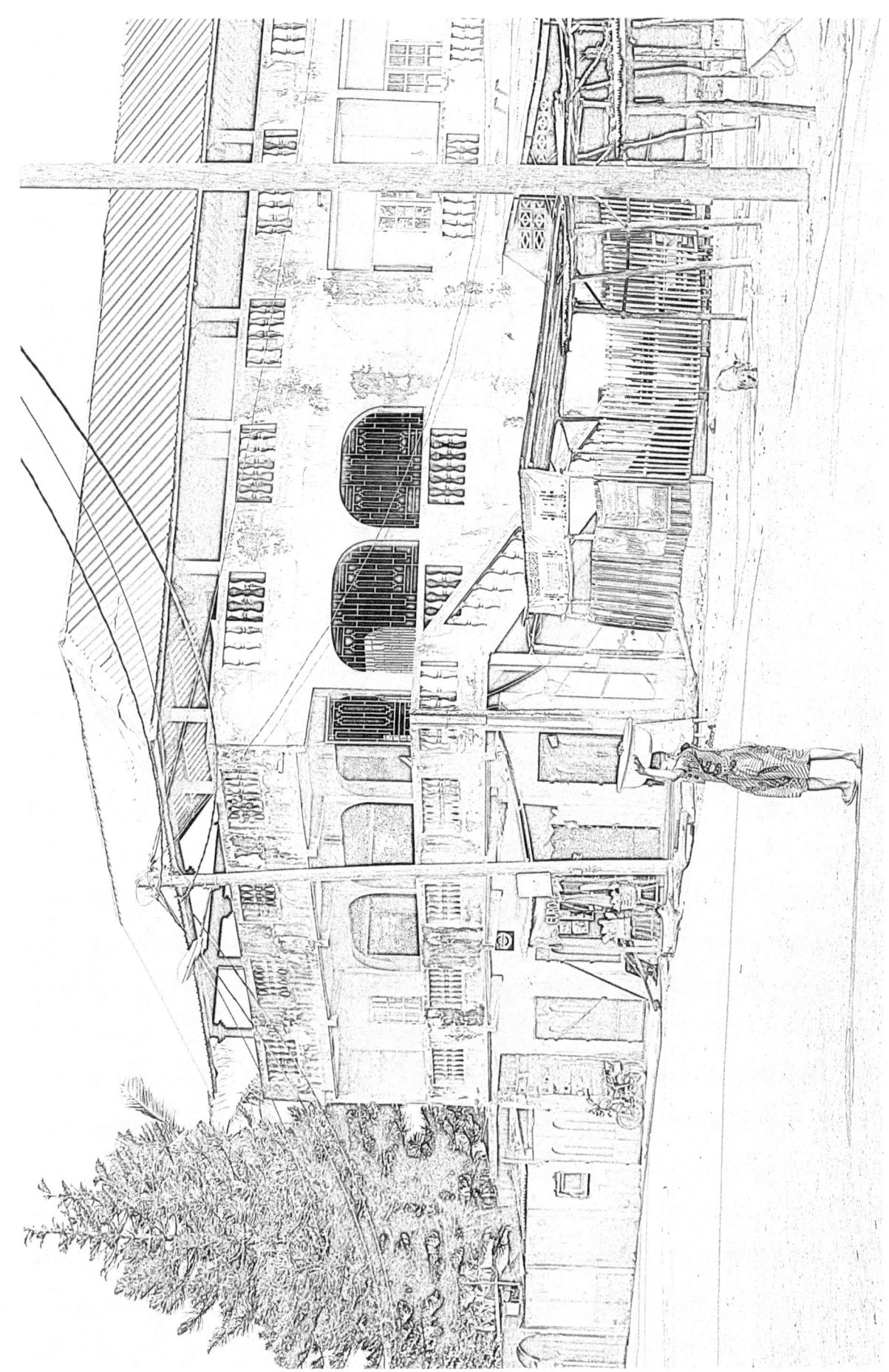

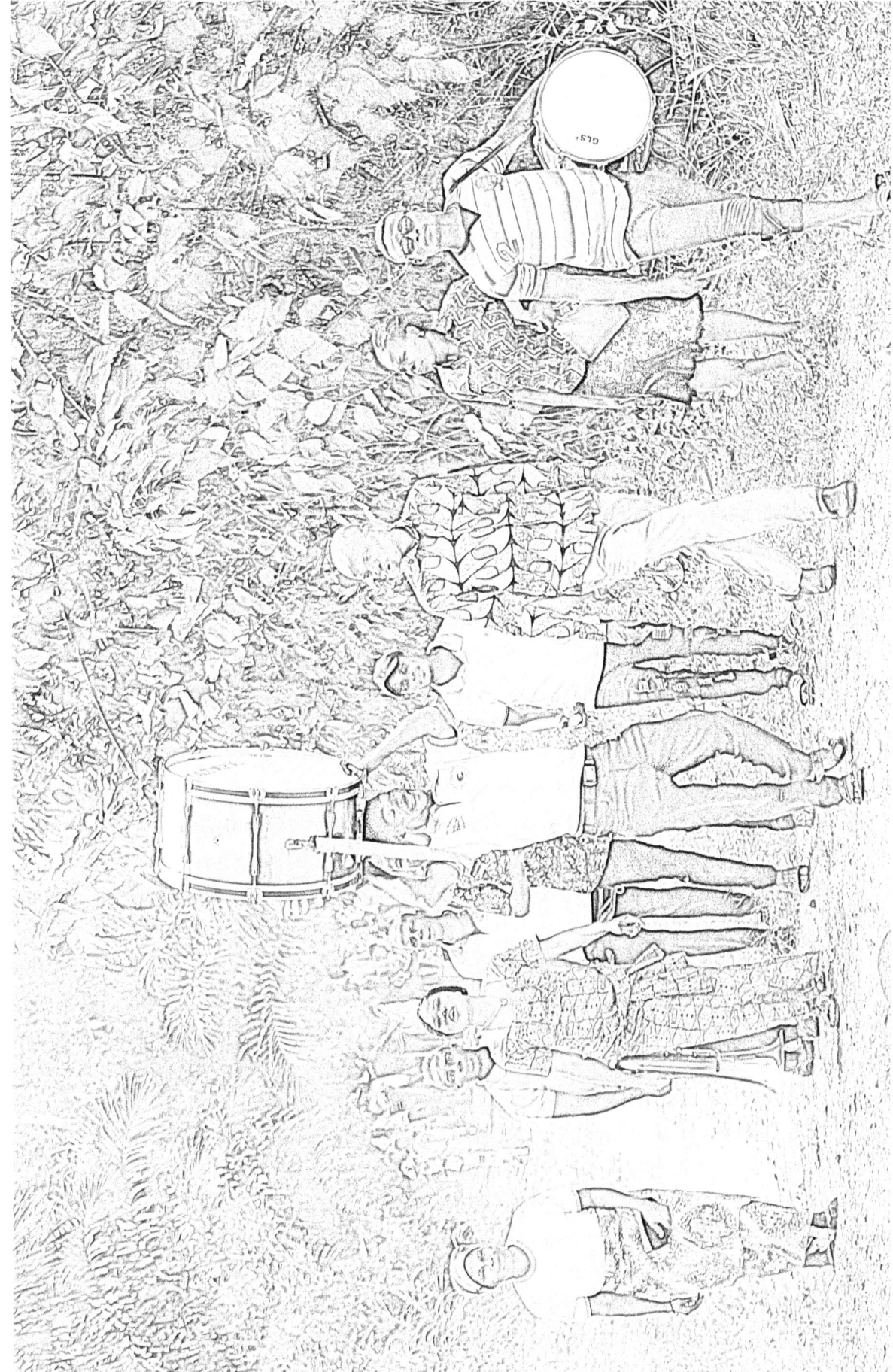

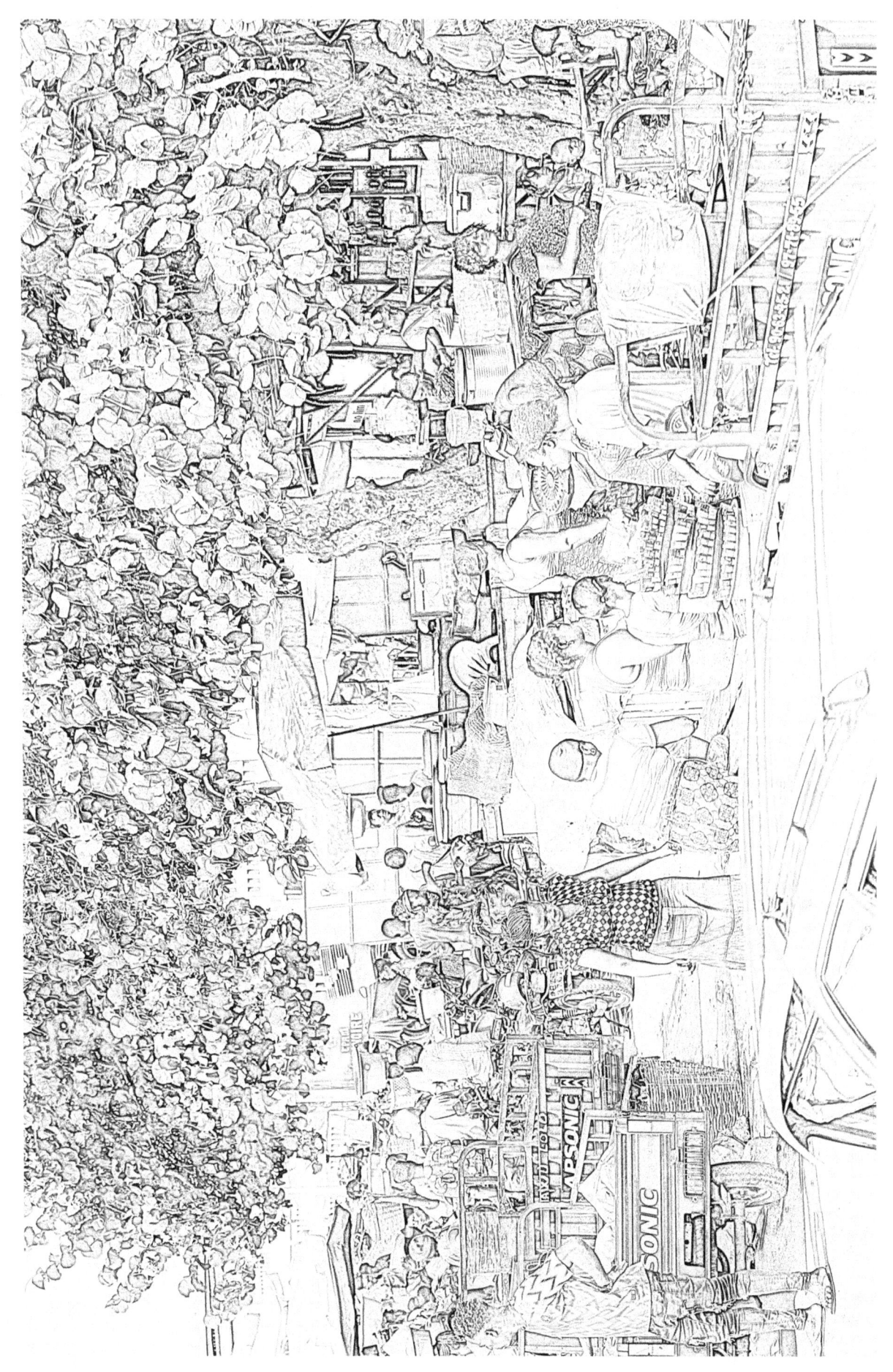

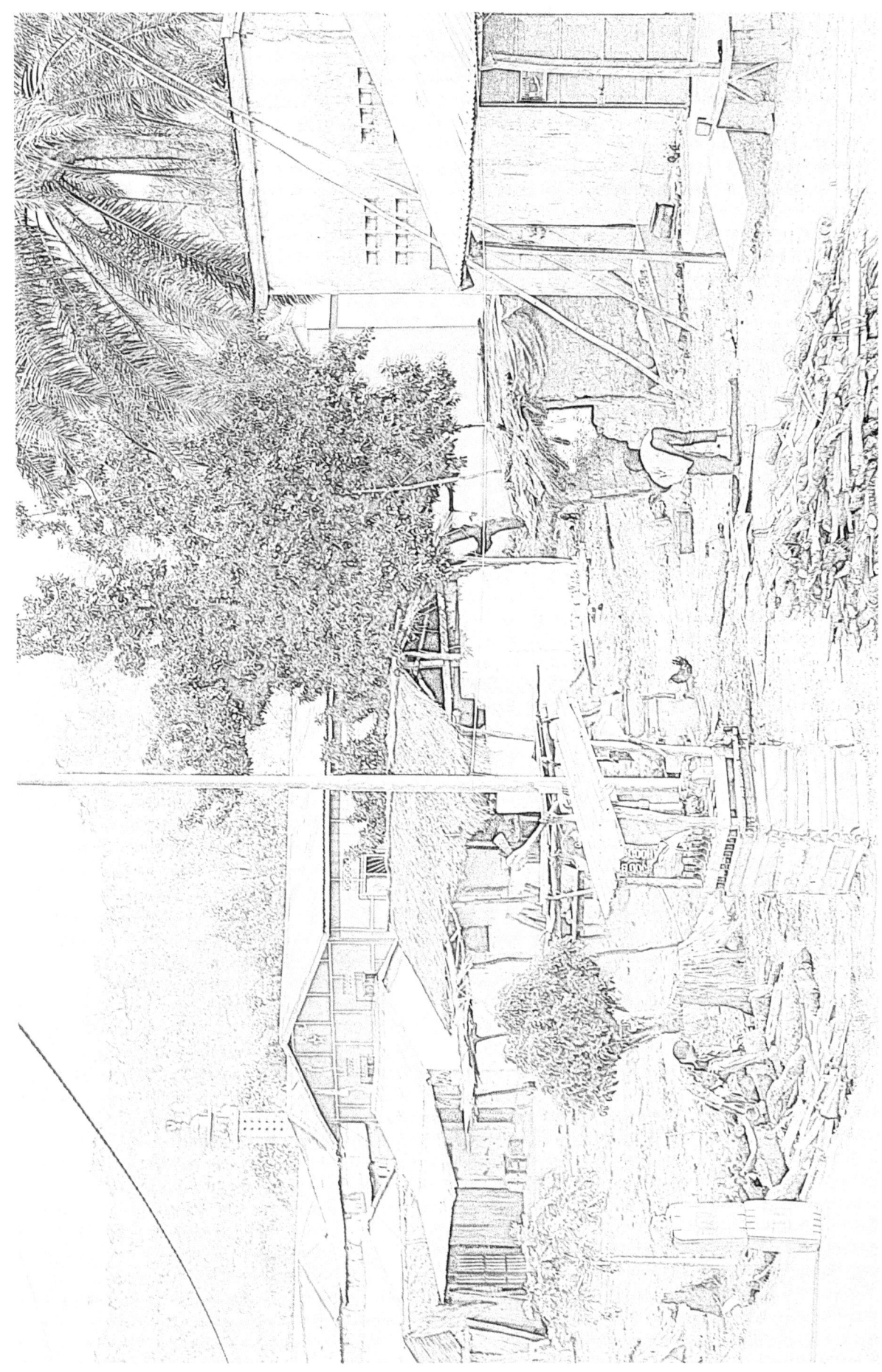

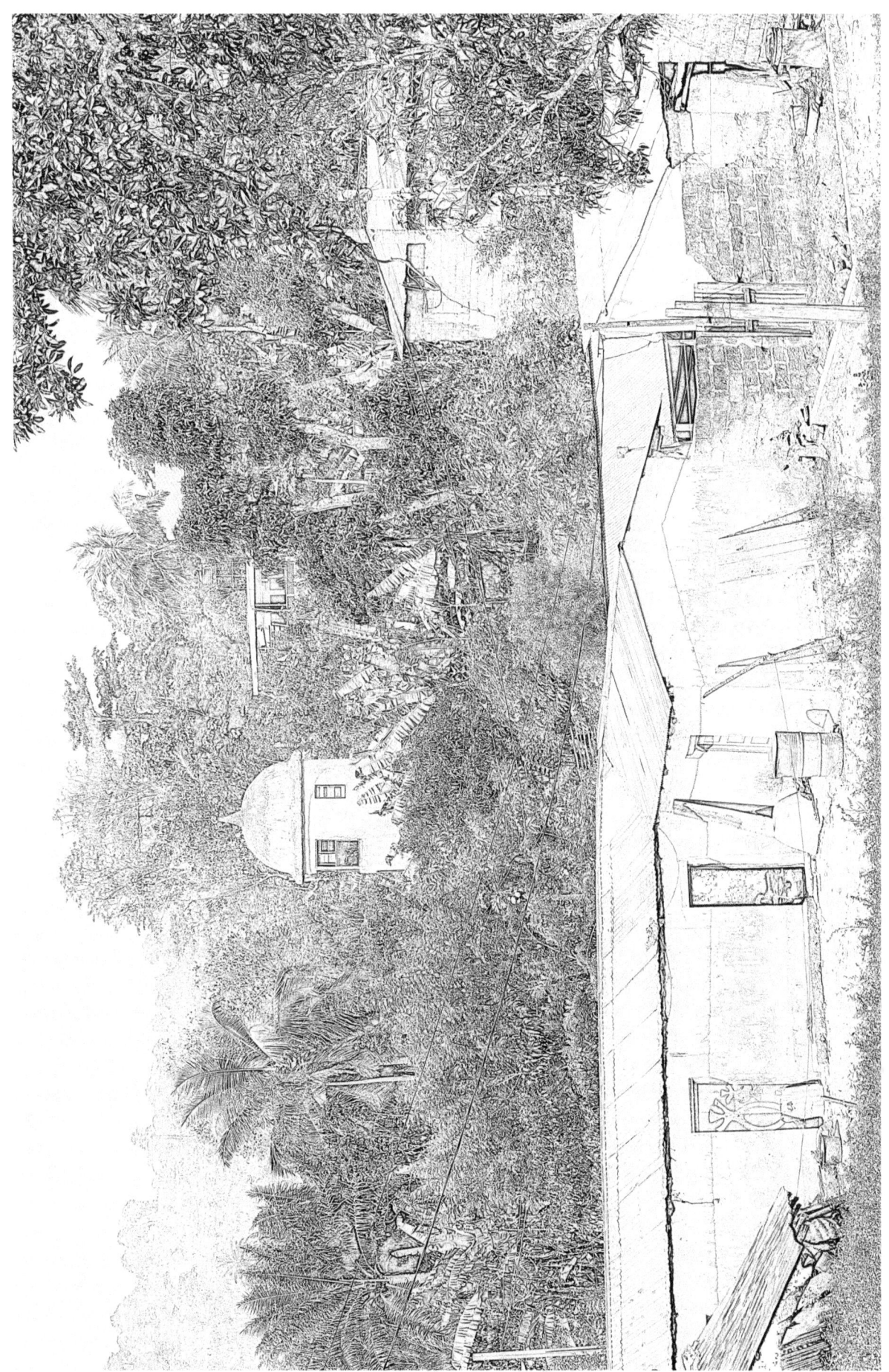

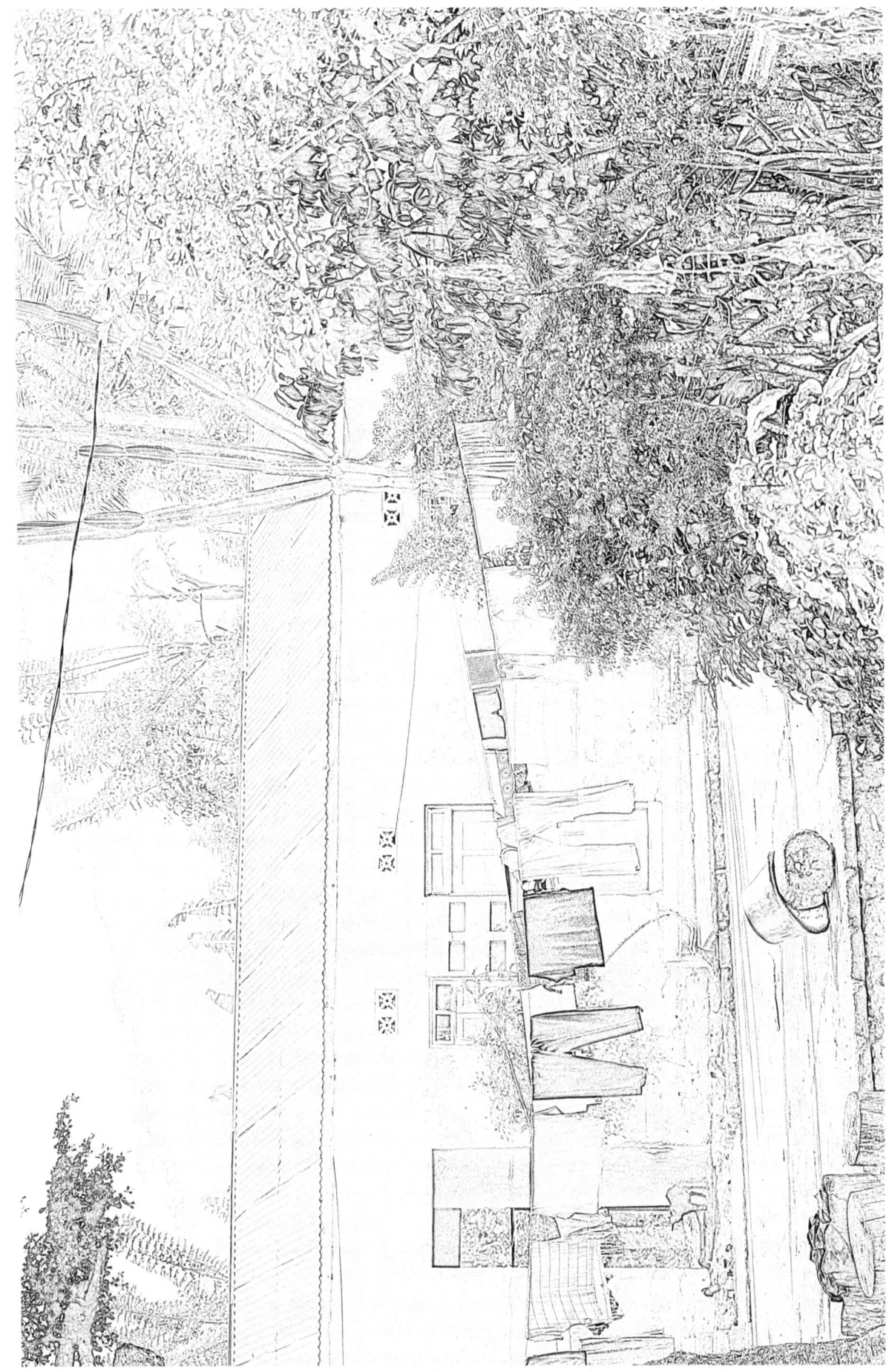

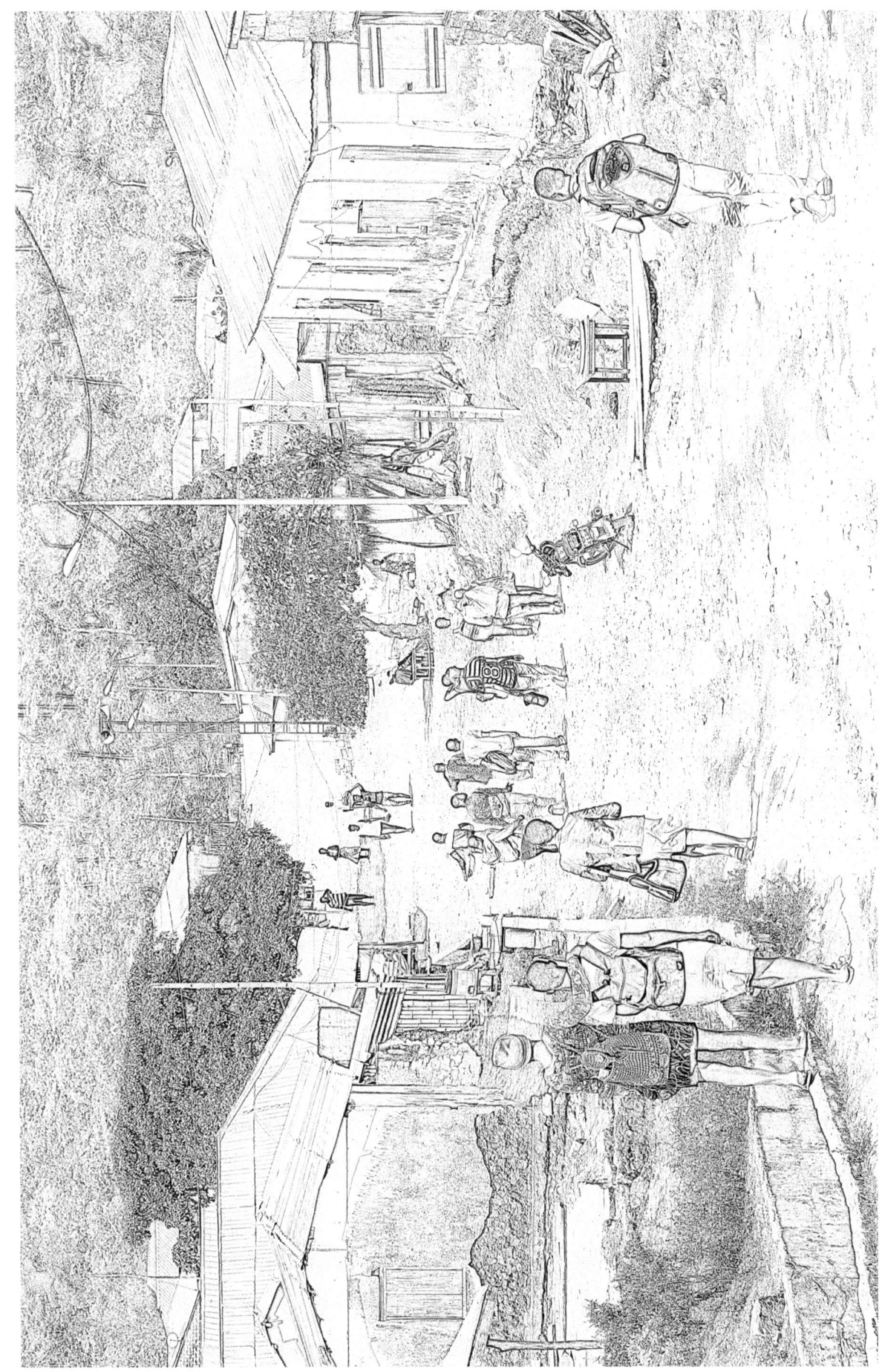

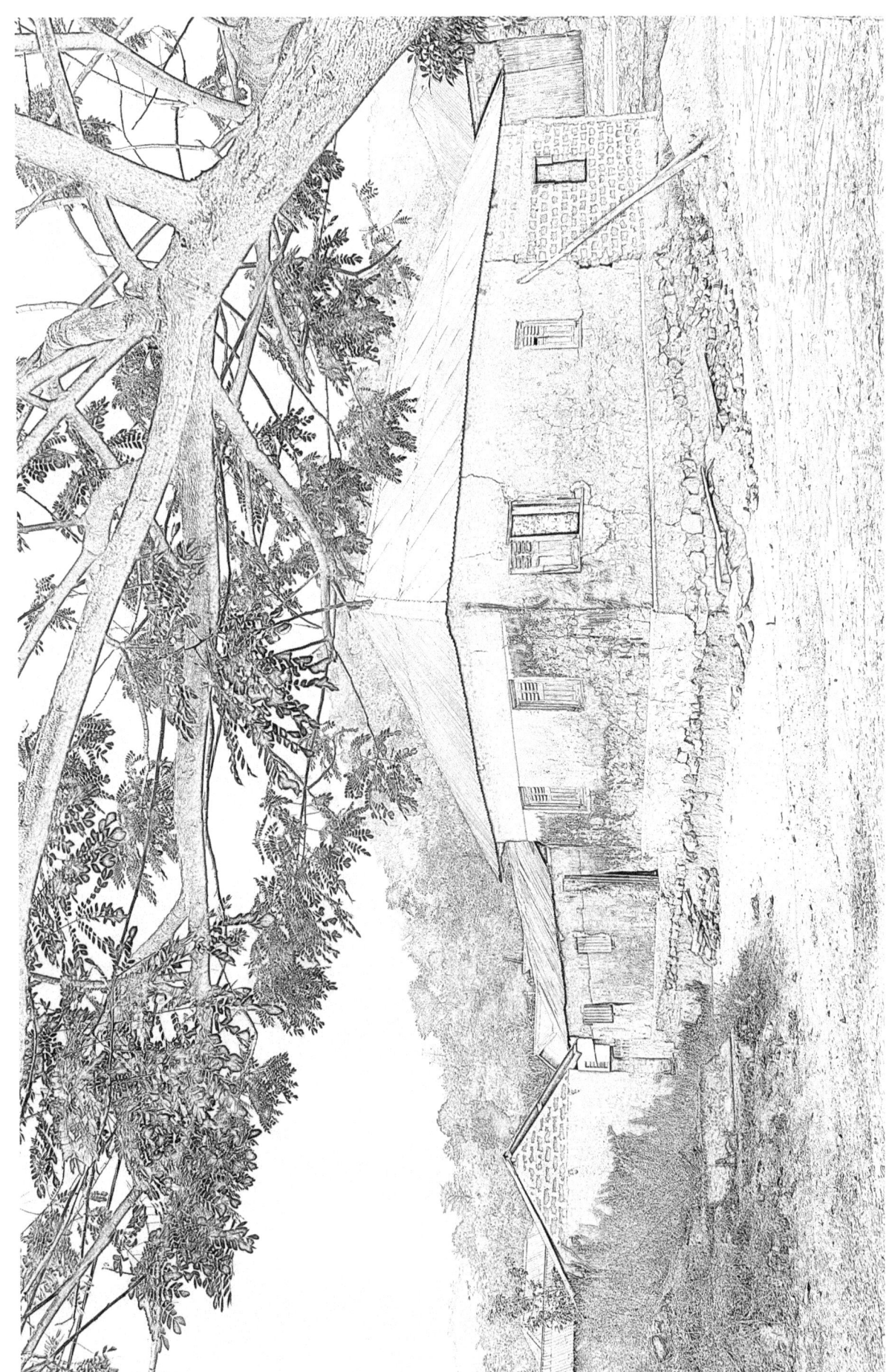

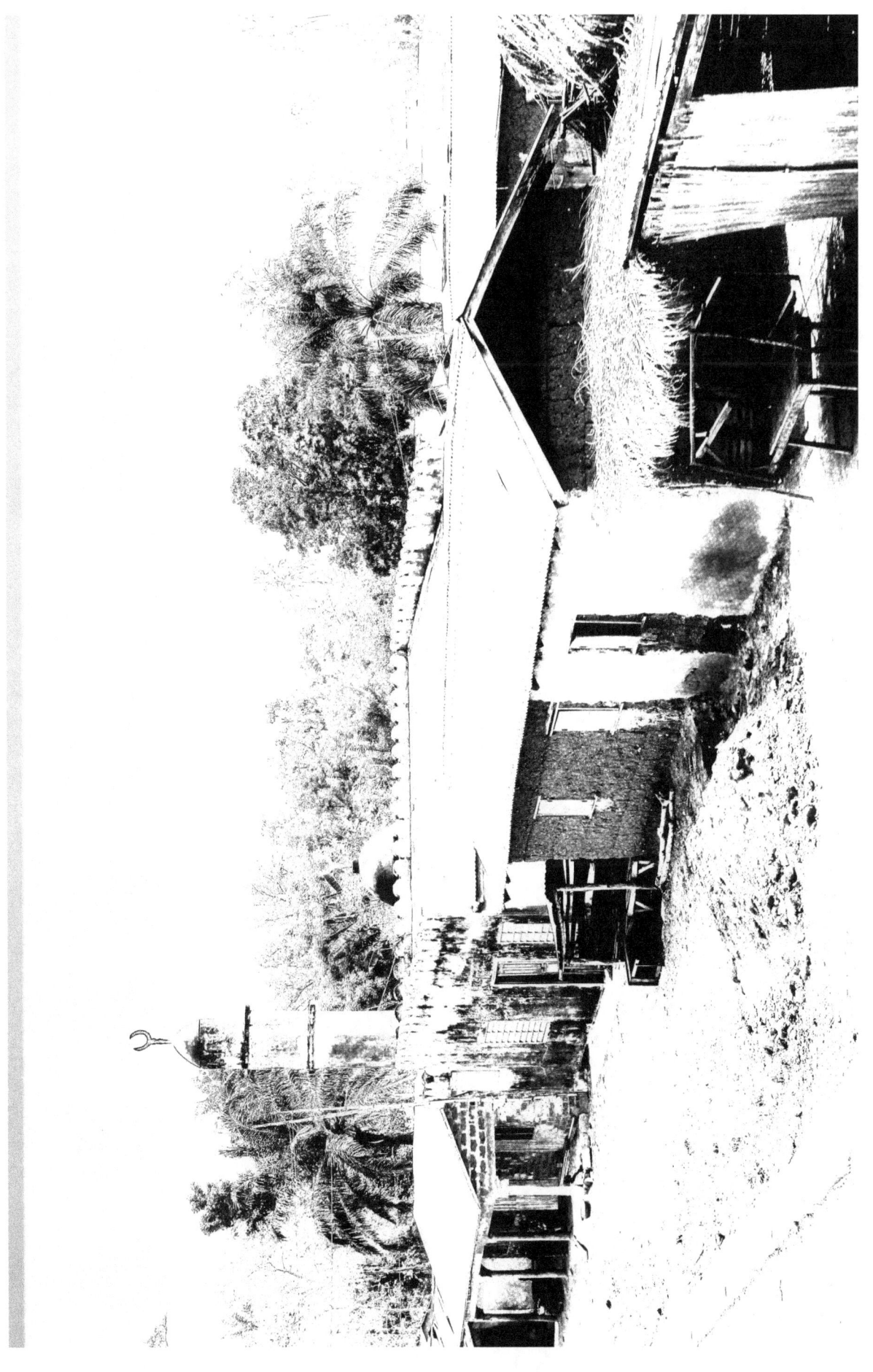

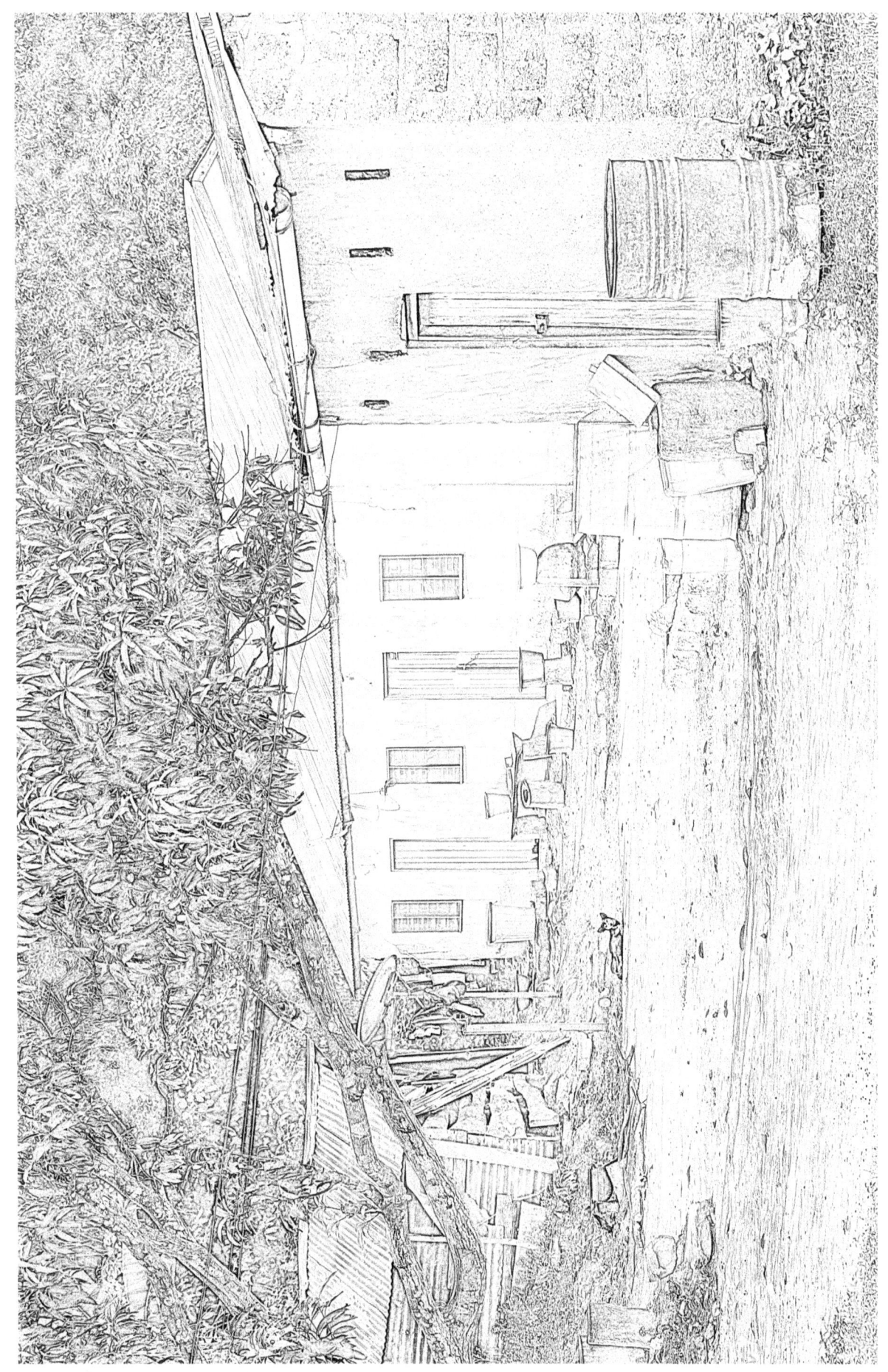

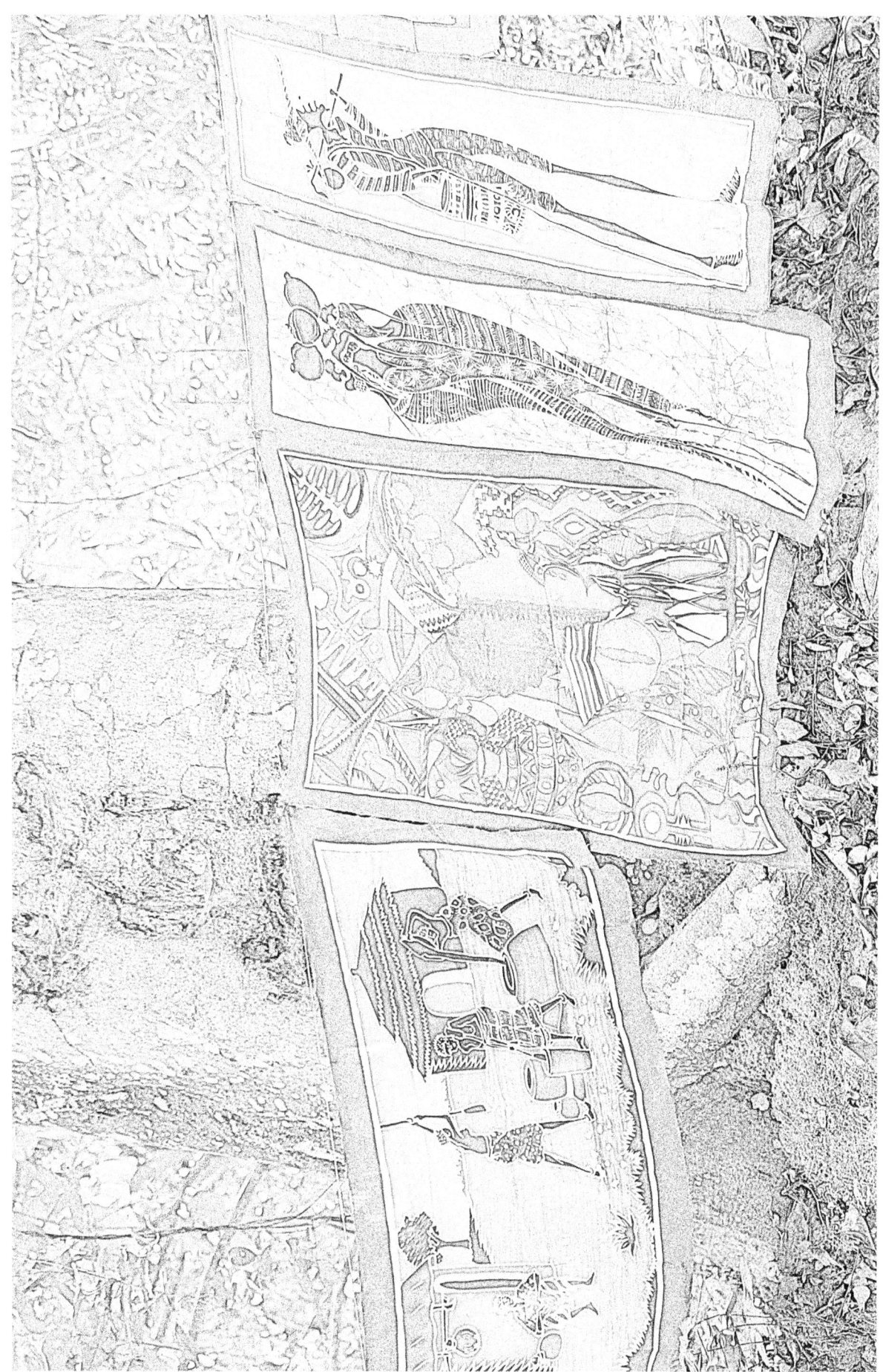

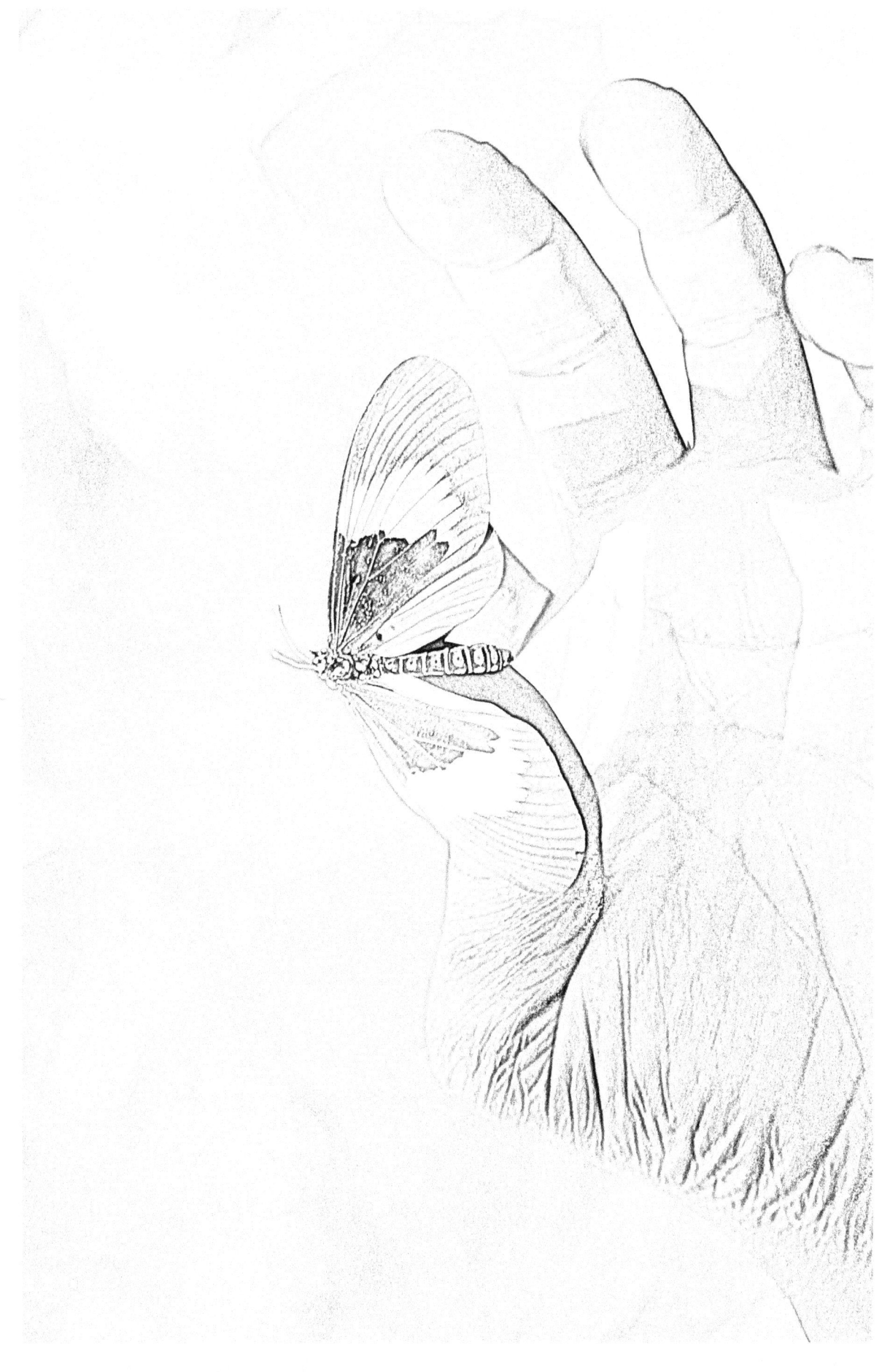

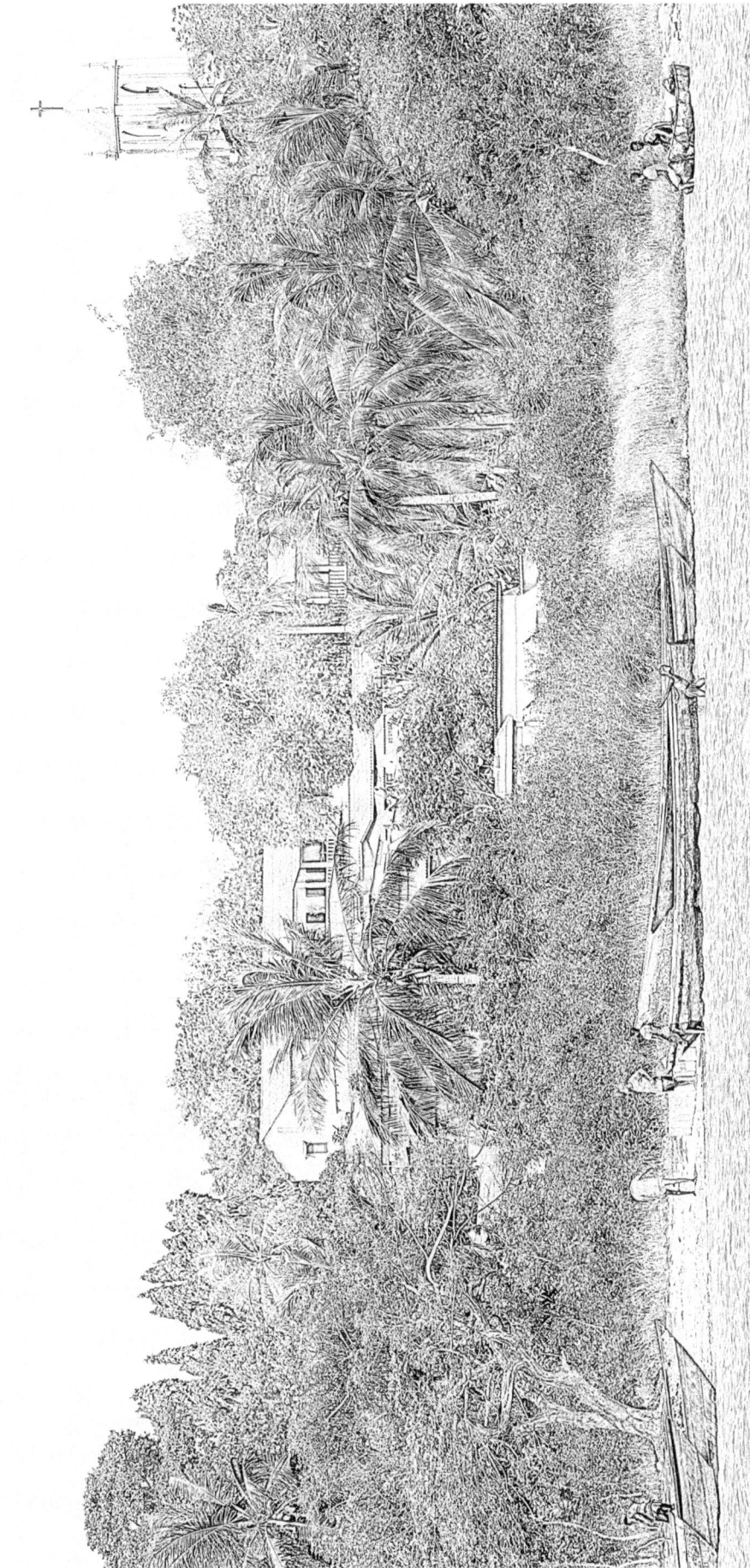

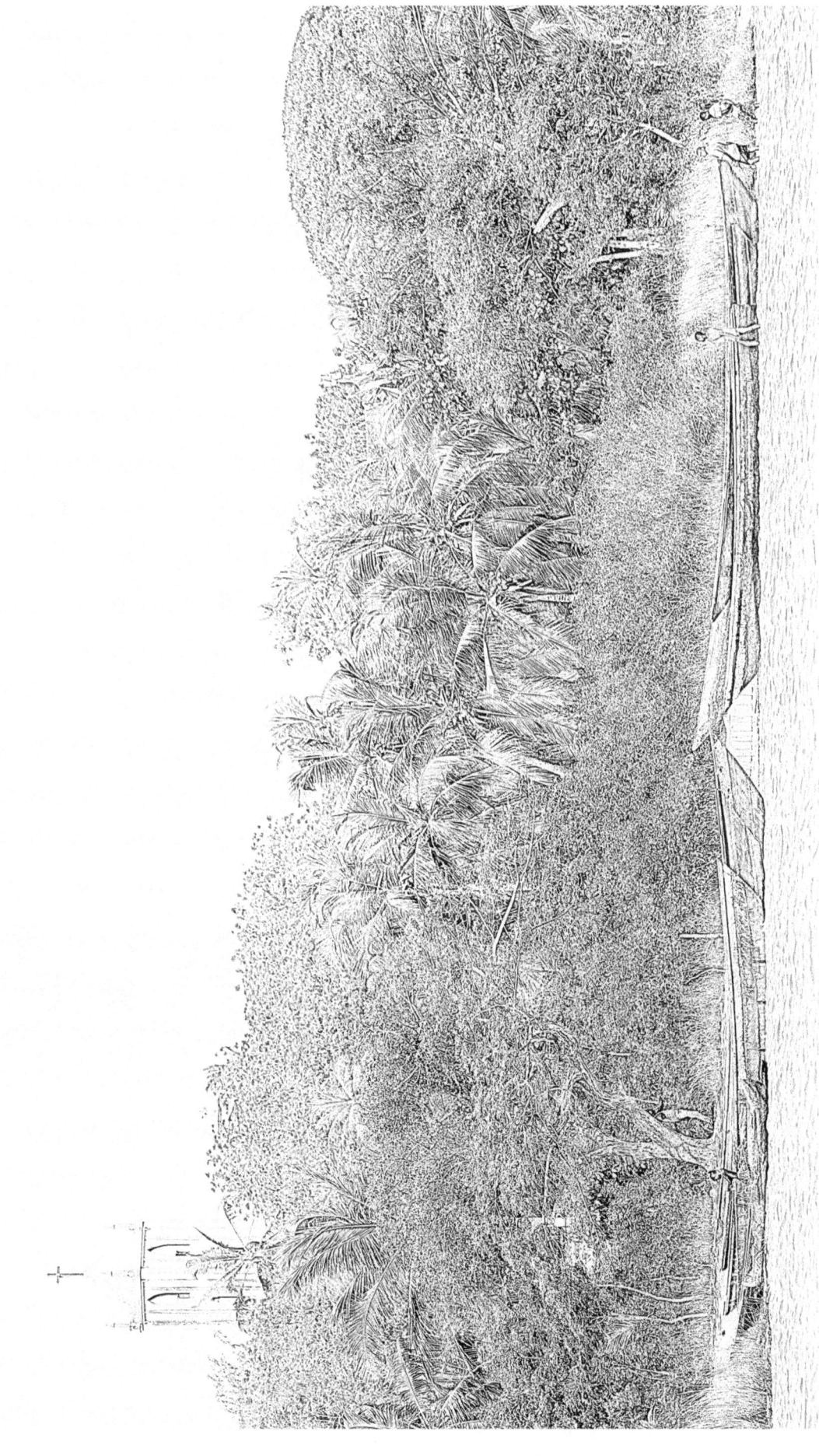

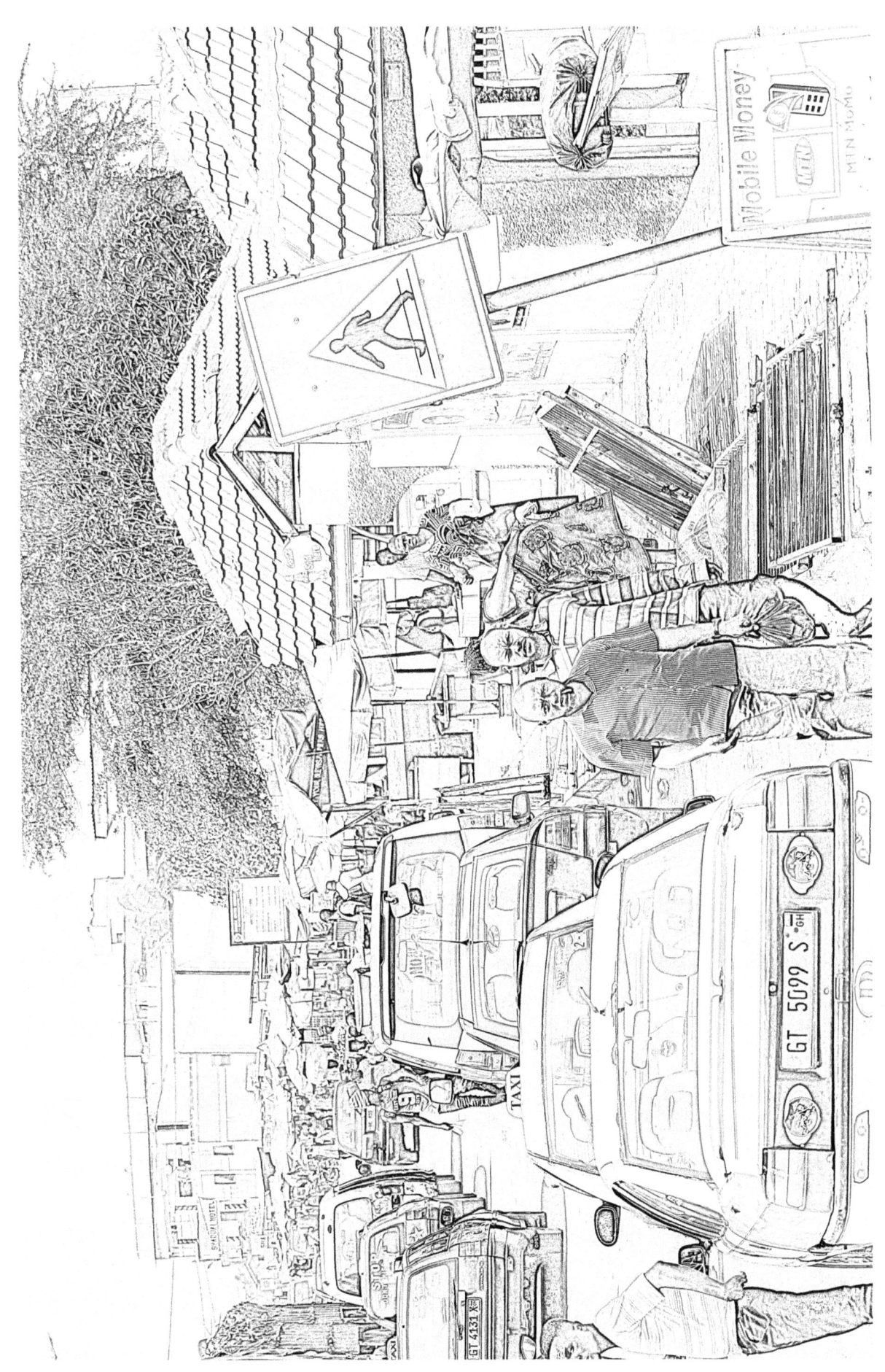

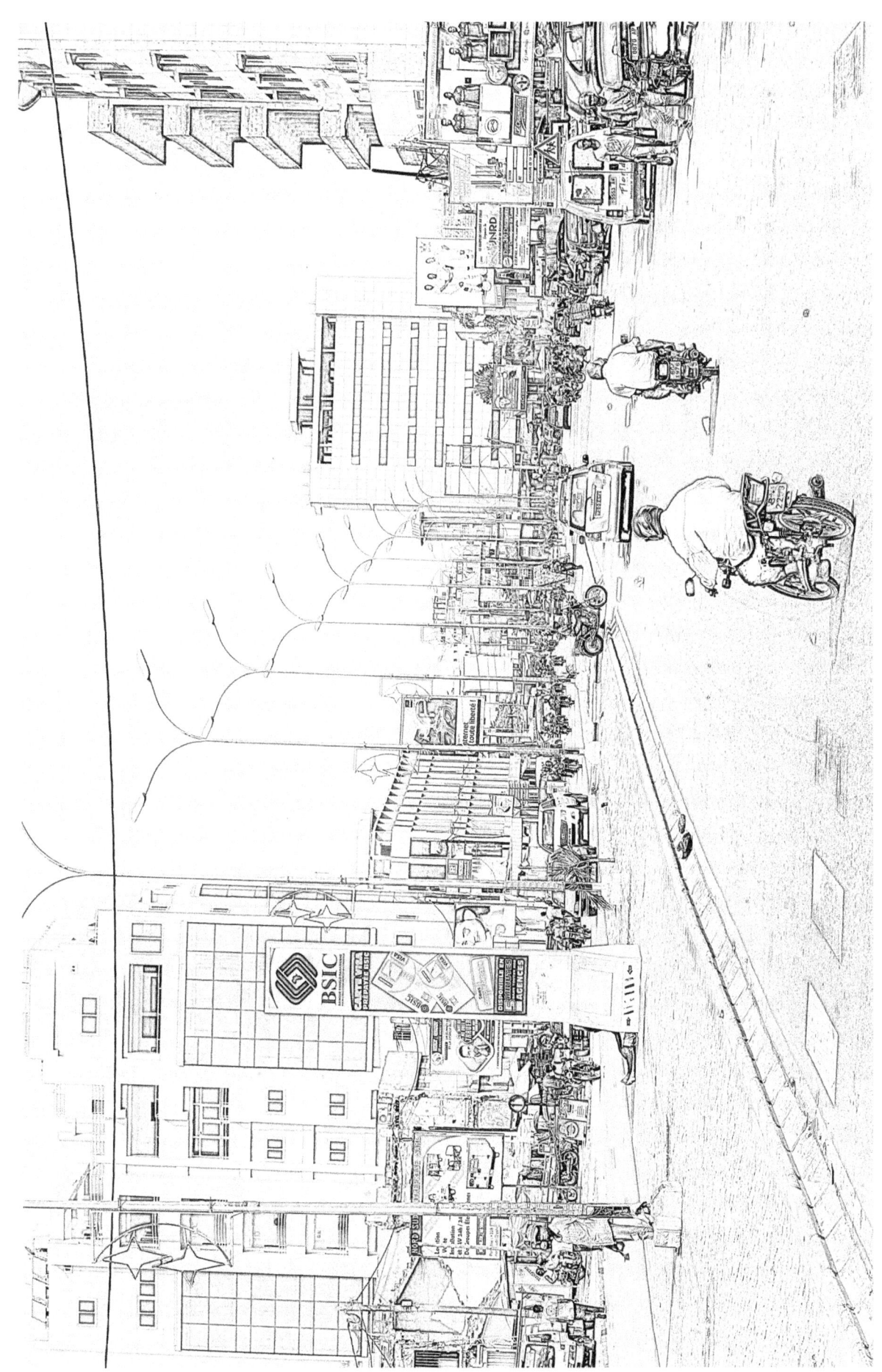

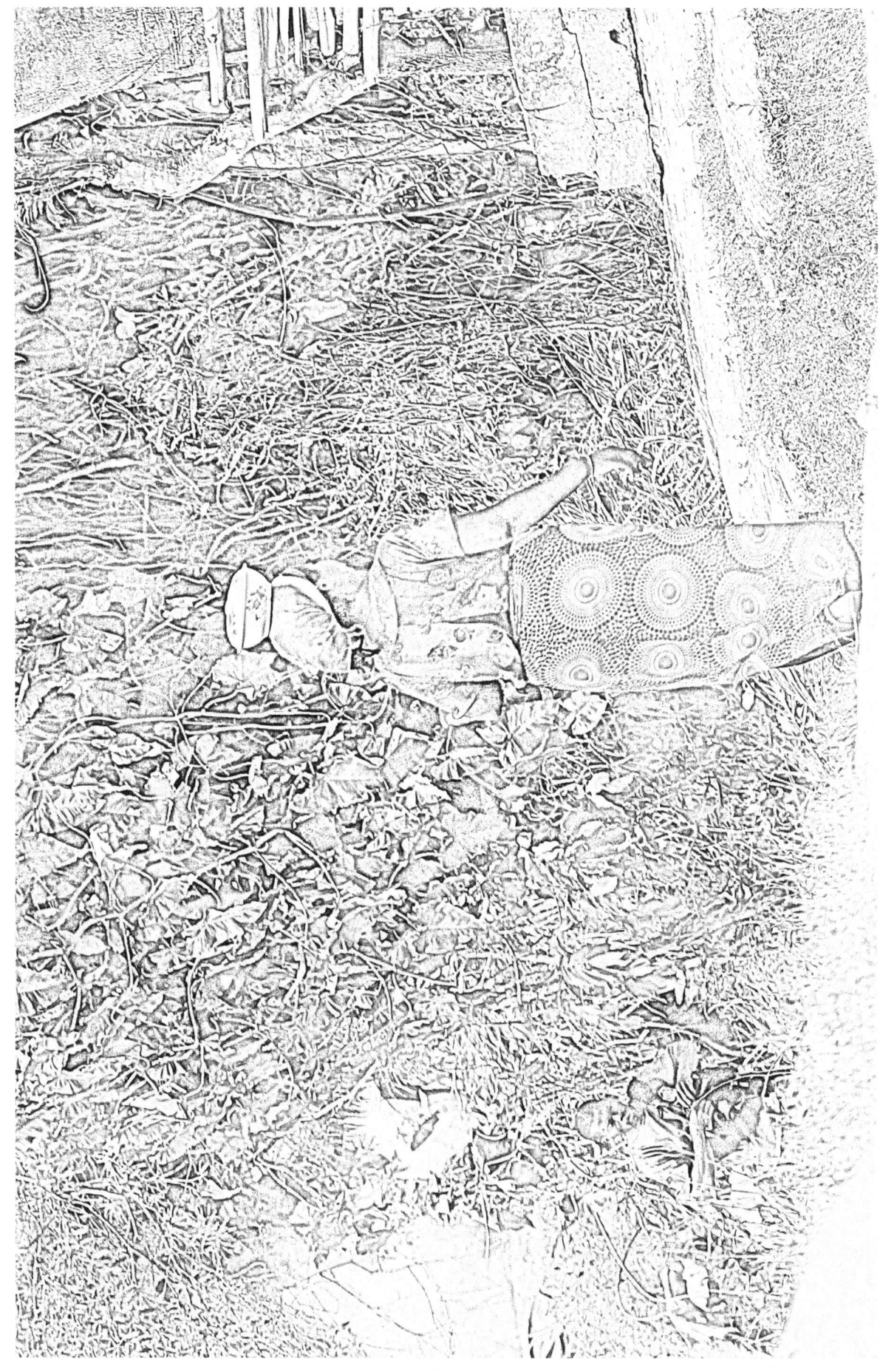

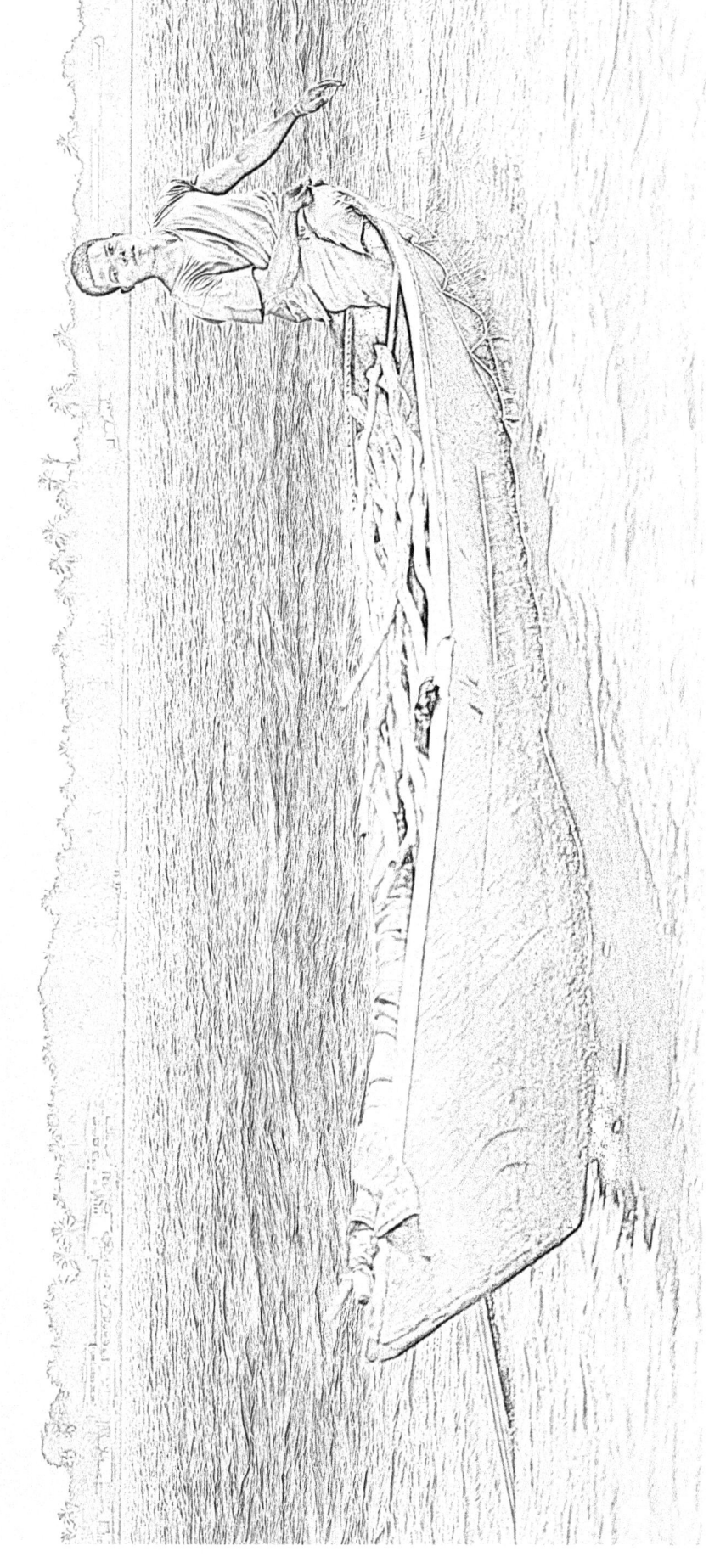

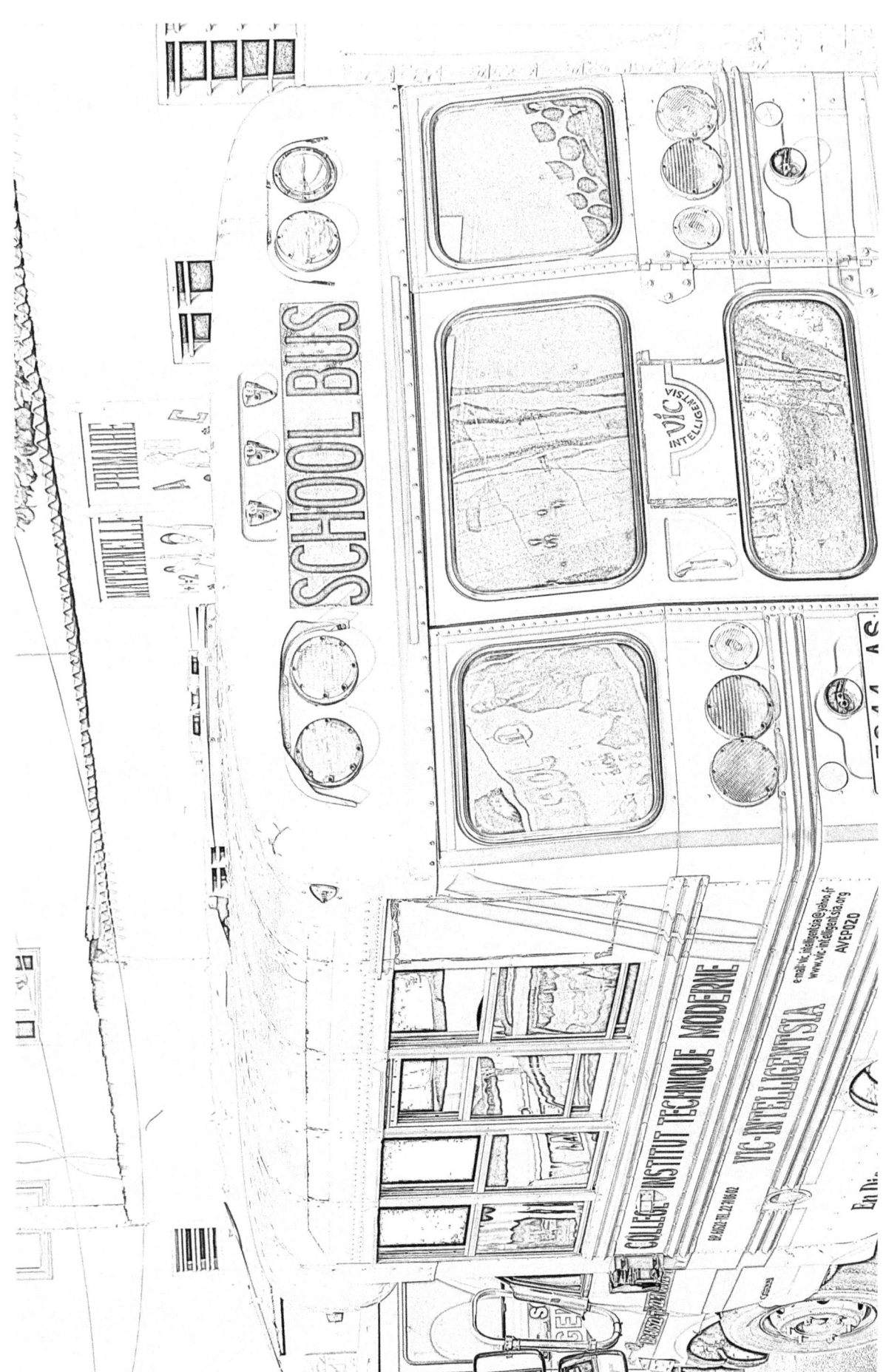

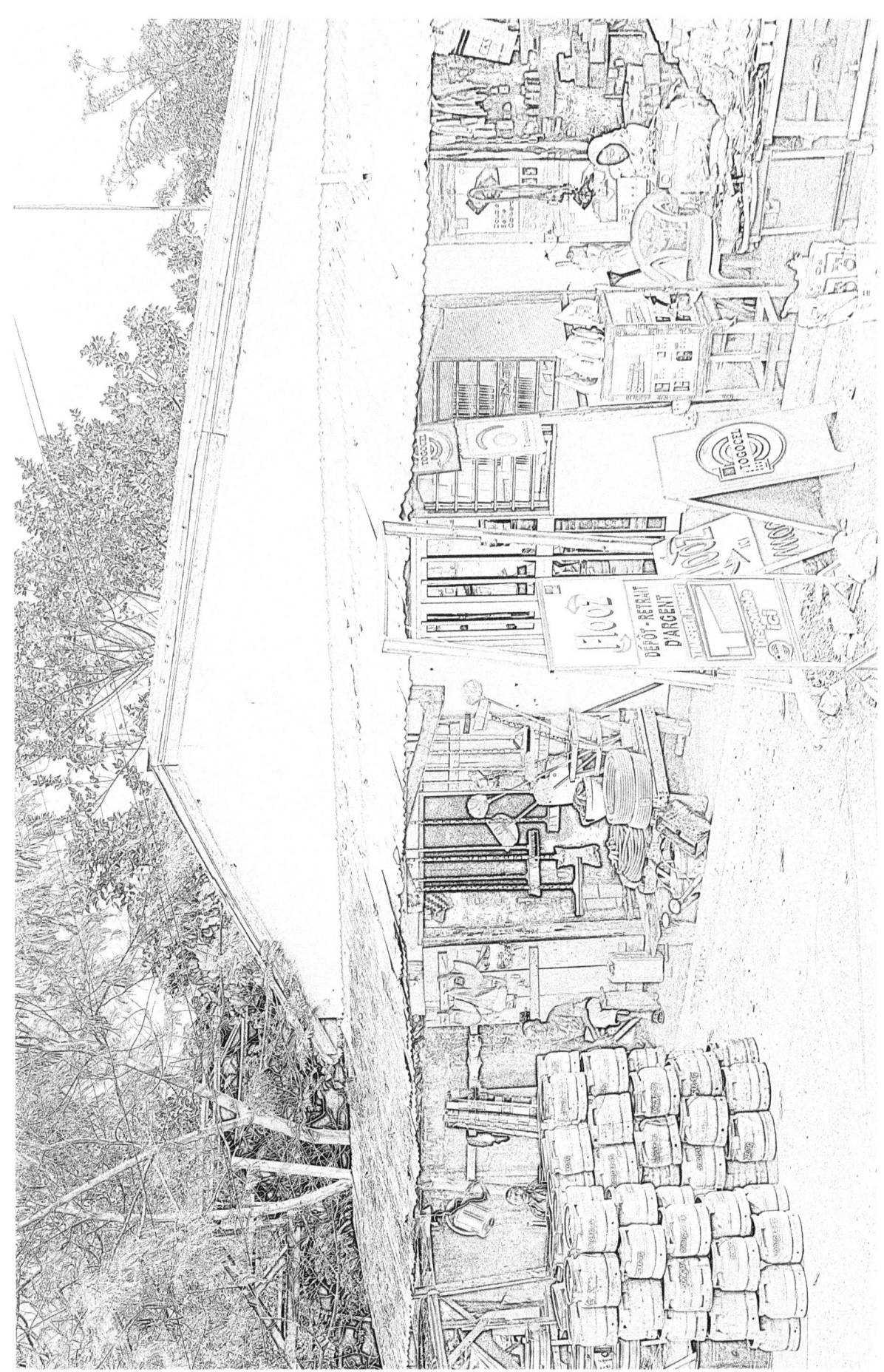

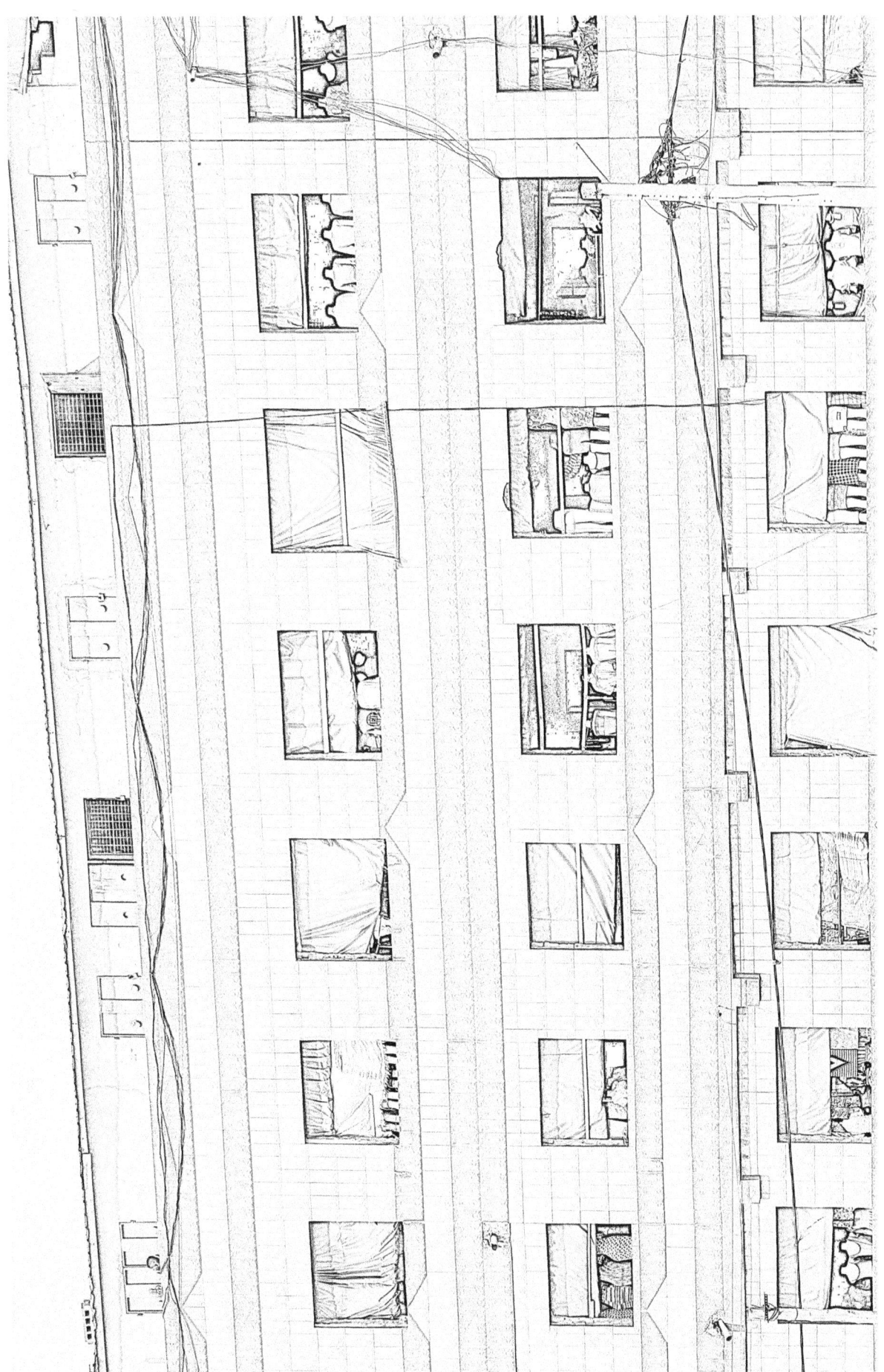

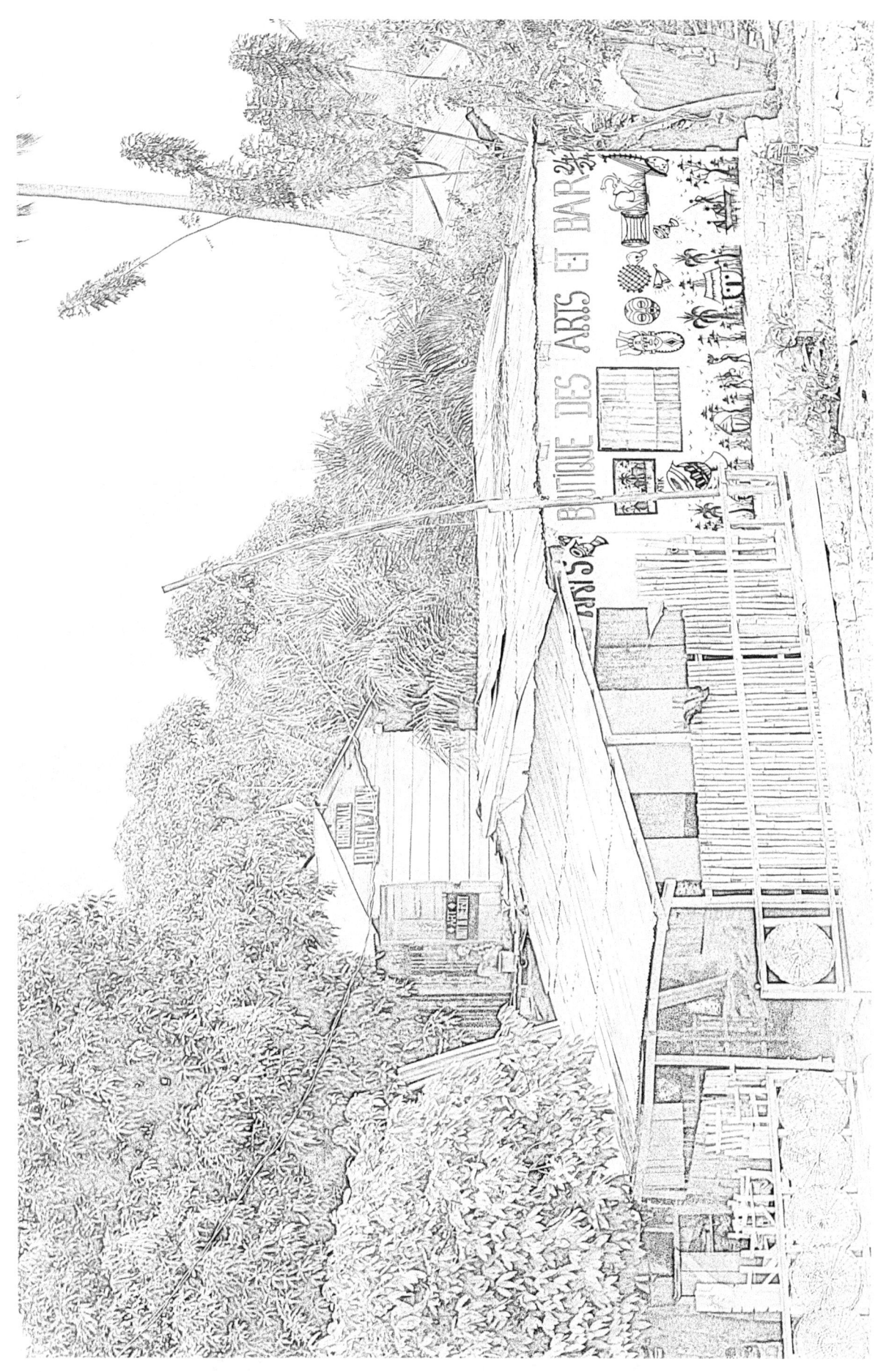

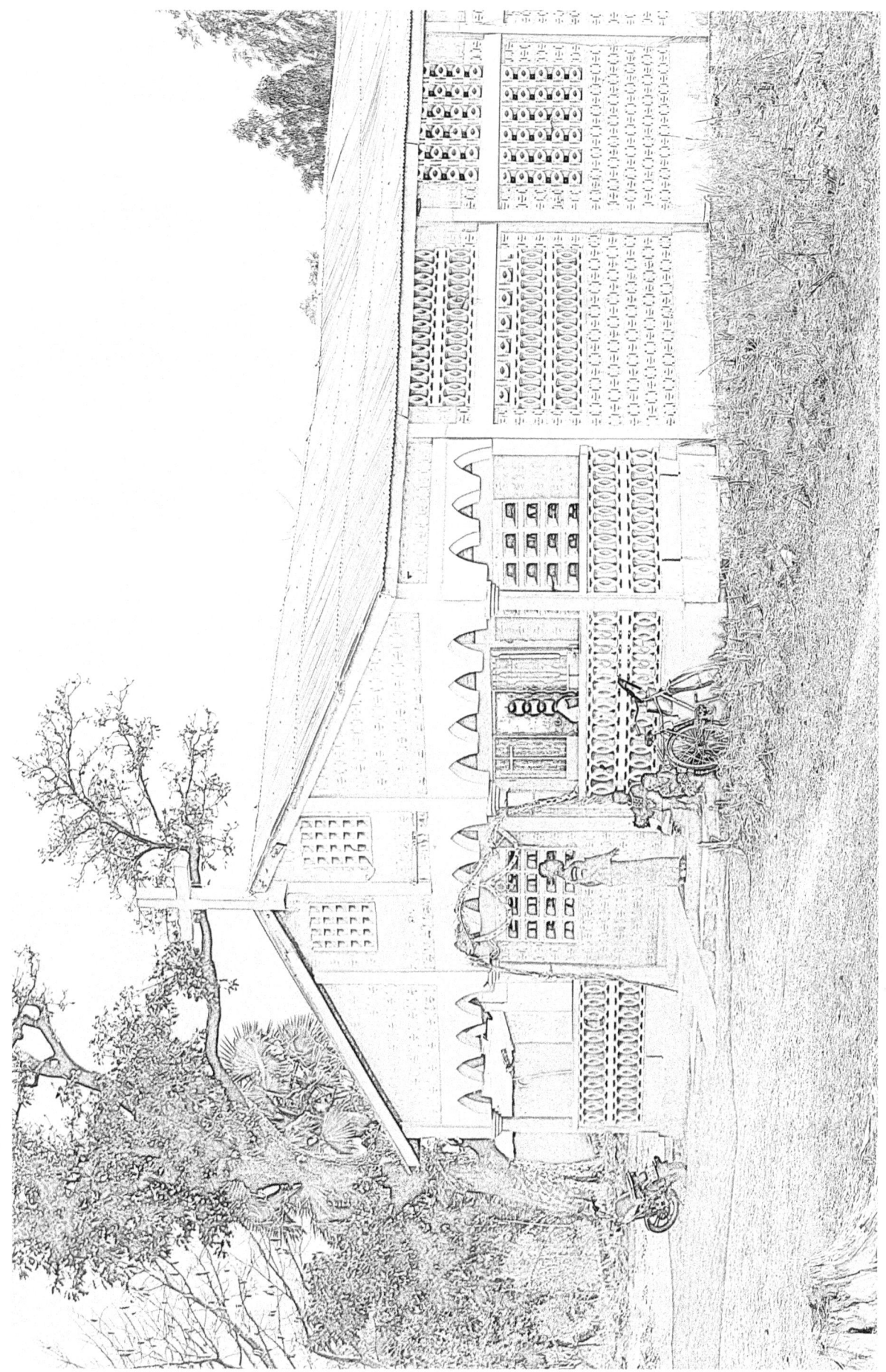

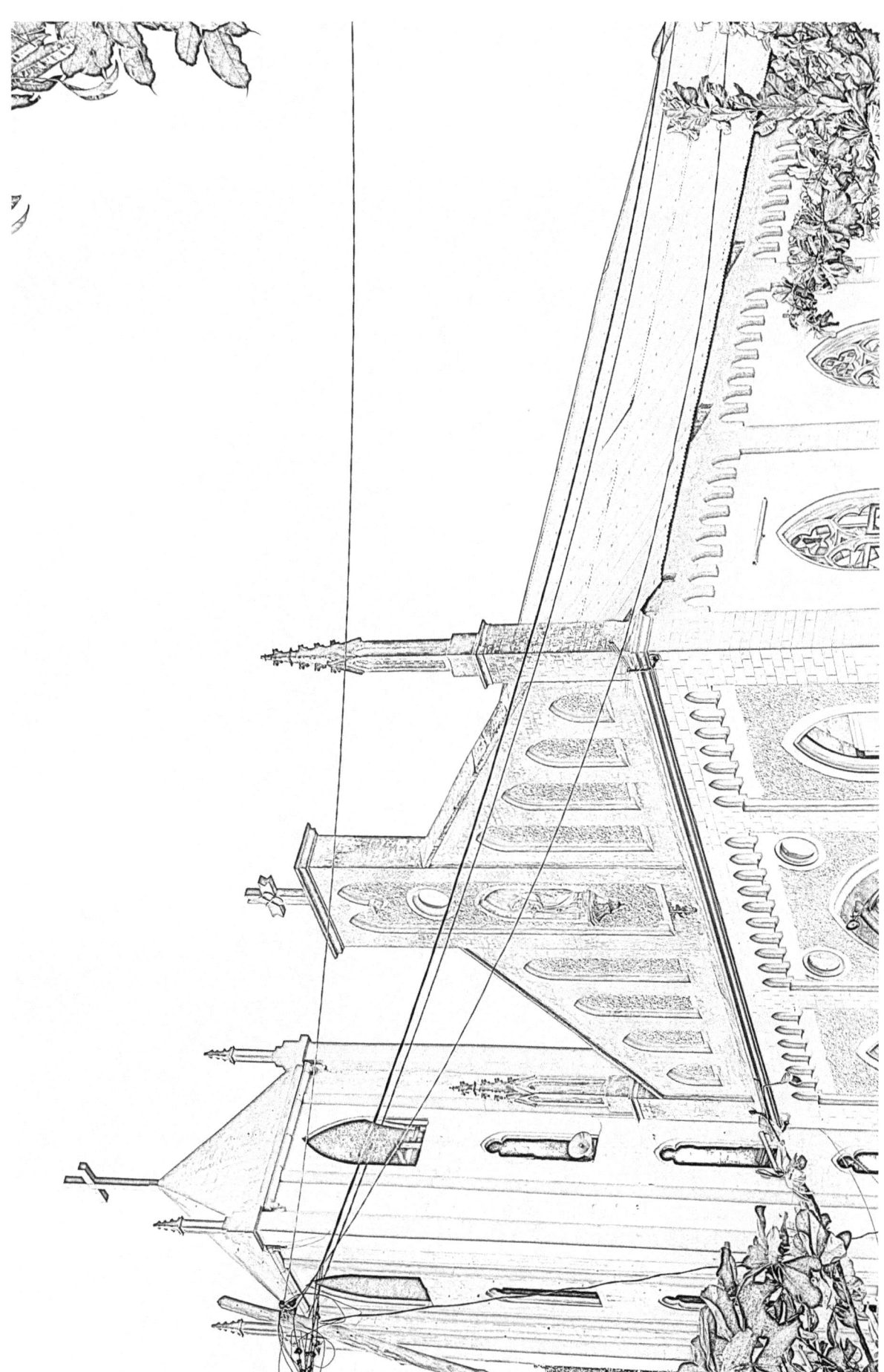

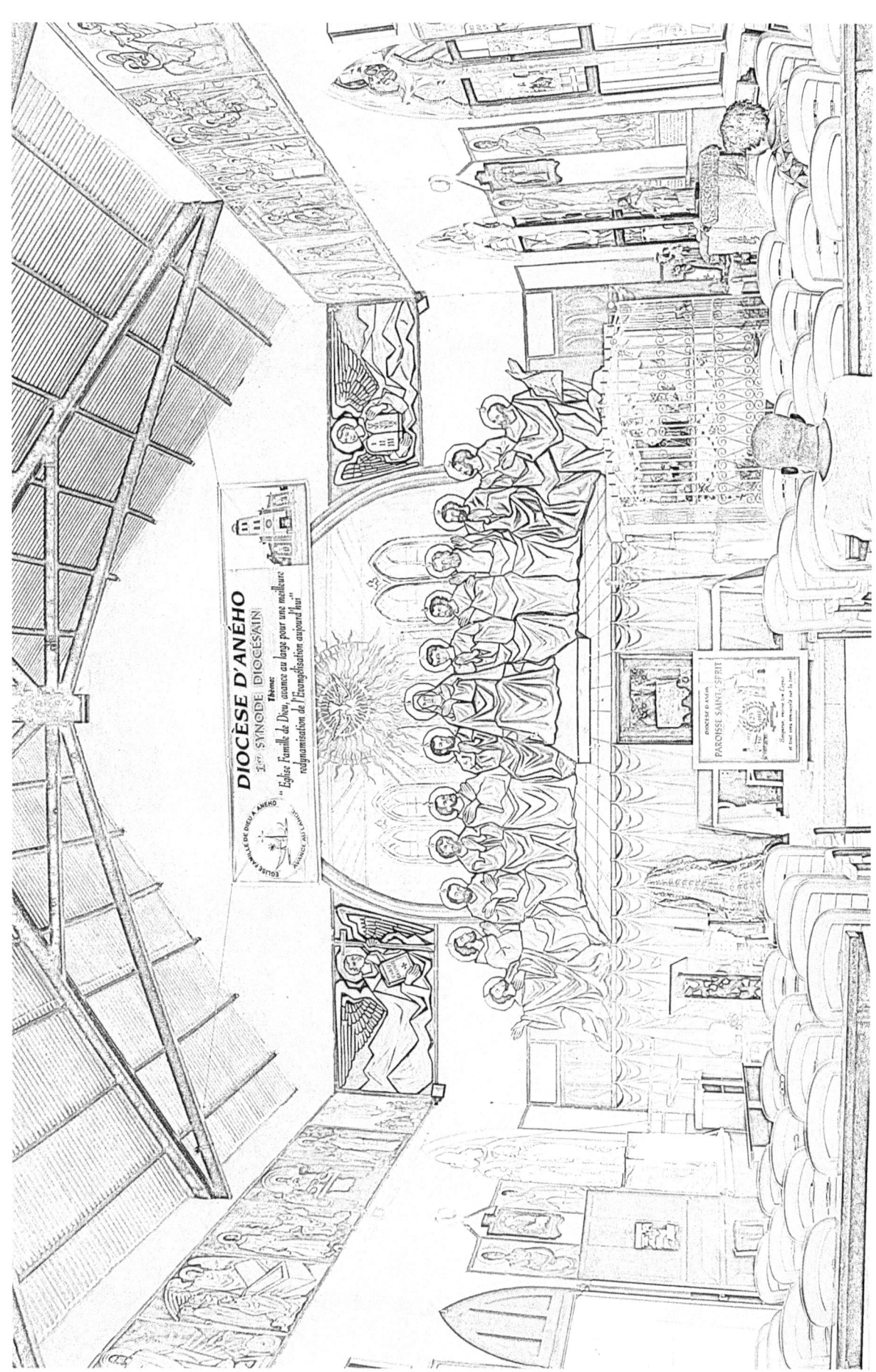

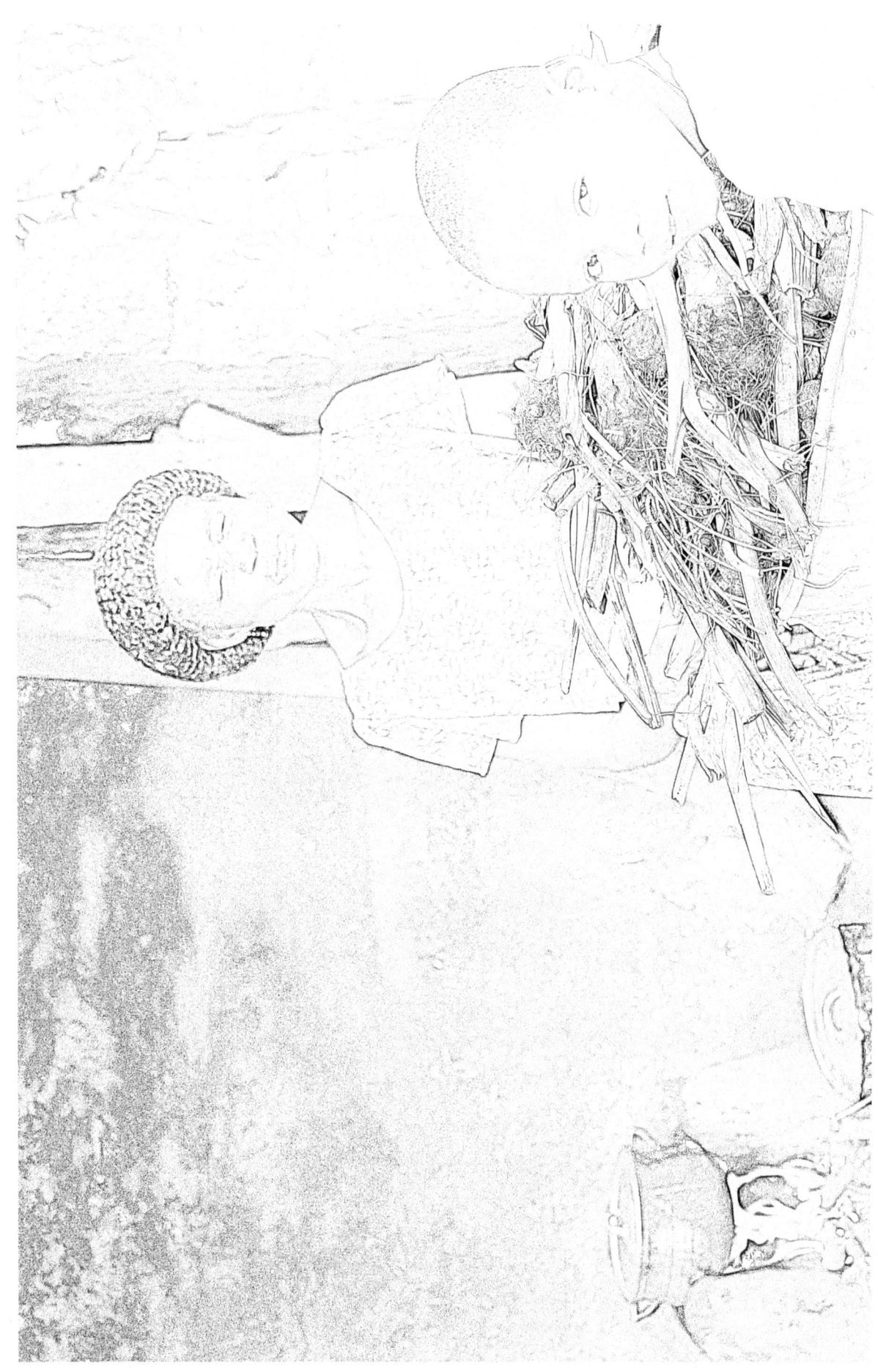